TWENTY - TWENTY
'ANNUS HORRIBILIS'

A JOURNAL
by
Dr. Maria H. Koonce

AuthorHouse™
1663 Liberty Drive
Bloomington, IN 47403
www.authorhouse.com
Phone: 833-262-8899

Because of the dynamic nature of the Internet, any web addresses or links contained in this book may have changed since publication and may no longer be valid. The views expressed in this work are solely those of the author and do not necessarily reflect the views of the publisher, and the publisher hereby disclaims any responsibility for them.

Any people depicted in stock imagery provided by Getty Images are models, and such images are being used for illustrative purposes only. Certain stock imagery © Getty Images.

This book is printed on acid-free paper.

ISBN: 978-1-6655-2568-8 (sc)
ISBN: 978-1-6655-2569-5 (e)
Library of Congress Control Number: 2021909988
Print information available on the last page.

Published by AuthorHouse 06/18/2021

authorHOUSE®

DEDICATION

TO OUR NEW GENERATIONS

Amanda and Brandon Turner and their three + children: Alahna, Elijiah, Nyjiah

Candice and Justin Griego and their two boys: Liam and Noah

Savannah and Brett Saxon and their two girls: Olivia Grace and Blake Rose

Madison Corley and Roberto Rodriguez

Brady and Lyndzi Schrader and their two boys: Branch and Bryar

Darby Schrader

AS WELL AS...

My brother Dr. Marcelo Haendel's children and grandchildren
My brother Eduardo Haendel's son, Nicholas
Bill's brother Bruce Koonce's children
The Corleys' kids: six girls and three boys +

All hard-working, studious, respectful, good, loving young people who make us proud in every way, and are a beacon of light and hope for the future... This chronicle of the unprecedented year may provide them with some insights and understanding of our society and our times.

<u>Note:</u>

"Annus Horribilis" = A year of disaster or misfortune in Latin
The phrase was used in 1891 to describe 1870, the year the Roman Catholic Church defined the dogma of papal infallibility.
Queen Elizabeth II on November 24, 1992 said "1992 is not a year on which I shall look back with undiluted pleasure. It has turned out to be an Annus Horribilis." She had lived through the separation of three of her children from their spouses and a fire in Windsor Castle.
I think **TWENTY-TWENTY** *fully qualifies as an* **'ANNUS HORRIBILIS!'**

Table of Contents

Introduction

Dr. Maria H. Koonce and William J. Koonce, MBA, MT

I first came to East Carolina University in Greenville, NC from Uruguay with an Exchange Student Fulbright Scholarship. In my first week there, I met Bill, my Gringo, and both our lives changed course. We married and had our first child in Uruguay, but returned to the United States to continue our studies. I became an educator in the areas of Foreign Languages and English for Speakers of Other Languages (ESOL), teaching in secondary and higher education institutions. Bill became an Engineer, and after twenty-five years he retired and joined me in field of Adult Education. He held two Masters' Degrees.

In 1976, we, with our two children, Michael and Maria-Paula, moved to Florida. I earned a Doctor's Degree, became an Adjunct Professor at Florida Atlantic University, and was appointed Coordinator of the Adult ESOL program in Broward County. I also represented the county in the Florida State Practitioners Task Force since its inception in 1996. This opened many doors for me as consultant, trainer, translator, and author. Some of my books include Loving the Gringo, A Bicultural Life, Retirement Rocks, Life's Rollercoaster, and An Extra/Ordinary Life. Bill and I delighted in our professional partnership, developing one of the levels of the New Reader's Press series English, No Problem, and conducting state trainings with interactivities and fun, which earned us the nickname of BATMAN AND ROBIN!

Since we both retired in 2007, we embraced our Golden Age, moving to a Retirement Community in Cocoa, undertaking a vibrant life-style full of new challenges, including world- wide travel and adventure. Maria-Paula and most of her family live across the state, and Michael is happy as a lark with his new family in Oregon. We are stronger in our ties to old friends around the globe and new ones in Lost Lakes, and to our remaining families in Uruguay, North Carolina and Pennsylvania.

Like for everyone else in the planet, 2020 was a very challenging year, but I recorded the events in a journal titled **TWENTY-TWENTY 'Annus Horribilis.'** This work resulted in a case-study, which follows a couple of seniors living through the unprecedented year: pandemic, political, social, and personal turmoil. The most devastating blow for me was losing my husband of 58 years. Now I remember and value our rich and wonderful past with the support of our son, our daughter, and the new generations that bring hope and light for the future.

Our activities

January 4 - Preparing for cruise in the Harmony of the Seas.
Bill started coughing and getting sick; I took him to Lake Nona VA Hospital; diagnosis: pneumonia and flu. (Hindsight: could it have been Covid-19?)
NO CRUISE FOR US!

- **January 7** - Returned home with oxygen: neighbors Paul and Michael helped him get in the house; Scott (our ex but forever son-in-law) came to help us settle in, learn about the oxygen use, and get us needed supplies from Walmart (like urine bottle).

- Bill began recuperating with approved VA support (nurses, physical therapists and occupational therapists); plus his primary care physician, Dr. Antoine, from the Viera Veterans Administration (VA) clinic.

- Maria Paula (our daughter) came to check up on us for a couple of days.

- **January 15** - I hosted book club in the Florida room, highlighting the Andes tragedy with the book ALIVE.

- Lily Wiggins and Mimi Sakal (old friends) came to visit; lunch at 'Lone Cabbage Inn.'

- Surprise neighbors BD party for Liz at Carol and Mike's house.

- Monthly dance at the clubhouse.

- Had the Hyundai Genesis serviced while having lunch at 'Kaye's' across the street.

- Baby shower for neighbor and friend Hazel's granddaughter in the clubhouse.

- Began my dental work.

- Took Bill to the Viera VA and Orlando VA for several appointments - he is not driving since his hospital stay.

- Normal activities, with some restrictions: since we are more homebound I decided to look into ordering new carpet for the bedrooms.

January 29 - Found out from respiratory technician, Frank, that Bill will continue to need oxygen; we began looking into buying a portable oxygen equipment, INOGEN, with our neighbor Bridget's advice.

In the news

In the meantime, an insidious threat was developing in China since 12/31/2019. If we saw in the news about the increased development of the Coronavirus throughout the first month of 2020, it would only have been to remember that we had visited the city of Wuhan, where this horror started.

Our activities

- Pretty close to normal routine, staying home and slowing down because of Bill's health: respiratory test indicated he will continue to need oxygen intermittently – disappointing news!

- New carpet ordered for the two bedrooms; only one guy shows up on the scheduled day, so it had to be postponed to the next day.

- Had also scheduled pressure cleaning the Florida room so had to have all stuff moved out; then we decided to change the carpet there as well; when we saw it new, clean, and empty, we also decided to buy new patio furniture: Bill selected a beautiful set from Lowe's.

- Restarting all electronic devices, with help from Spectrum and our technician, Bob Beck.

- Scheduling and waiting for deliveries and pick up...

- Researching INOGEN.

- Lunch with Nancy Lucas and Jean Anderson (colleagues and friends) in 'Squid Lips.'

- Continued appointments for my dental work, hair, nails.

- Book Club meeting in the Clubhouse.

- Worked on 'Out of the Mouth of Babes,' a collection of the granddaughters' quotes; this led me to pursue the search for appropriate photographs from the 90s, which Bill and I enjoyed for the umpteenth time.

In the news

More and more alarming: **2/2** first death outside China in Philippines; **2/8** first U.S. person dies in Wuhan, **2/13** the World Health Organization (WHO) names the Coronavirus Covid-19; **2/14** a Chinese tourist dies in France; **2/19** Diamond Princess begins disembarking passengers in Japan after long quarantine; **2/26** Pence is put in charge of the Coronavirus issue in the U.S.; **2/29** first death in U.S. in Washington state.

Our activities

Because of the necessity of clearing out rooms for the replacing of carpets, pressure cleaning and new patio furniture, we ...

- cleaned out closets;
- listened to old records;
- had lunches in the lanai, basking in beautiful Florida weather, with our new patio furniture;
- enjoyed looking through our photo albums;
- one visit from Maria Paula for lunch when Bill cooked a 'parrillada' on our new electric grill, not being allowed to be around an open fire because of the oxygen.

Our activities

- Sitting outside enjoying the new carpet and furniture, we noticed an increasingly foul odor; turned out there was a dead opossum under our house: $175 to remove it and $325 to fix the damage and replace whimsy metal covers for enclosure.

- Continued medical care with tests and doctors' visits in Viera, until they cancelled all non-essential visits and began communicating by phone.

- Continued home care with physical therapy twice a week.

- Ordered Portable INOGEN which was delayed and finally delivered 10 days later on a Friday evening at 6:30 pm by UPS; Bill charged one battery and when he plugged in the second one and sat to dinner, we started hearing alarming 'beep,' 'beep,' beeps;' saw smoke coming out of the machine and smelled an electric burn-smell. Frustration over the weekend and back on the phone with Jessie, the sales person and other contacts of the manufacturing in California to finally get the replacement and begin, very cautiously, using the portable.

- **March 12** - Had an after dinner get together with about 15 friends. The last one for the year before the 'shutdown!'

- We went to *Bill and Anne Coleman's; only six of us, to celebrate St Patrick's Day.

- A couple of days after the Lithium battery scare, I was sitting in the kitchen having placed a potato in the oven for Bill's dinner, when I heard an explosion; even after turning off the oven, a small electric fire persisted on the heating element, and had to resort to the fire-extinguisher that Scott had bought when we brought Bill from the hospital and the oxygen supplier insisted we should have one in the house. It did put out the fire, but the powder invaded the kitchen and the entire house. Unfortunately, Nancy (our cleaning lady) had just done her thorough cleaning, so this time it was my turn to spend the next few days removing the evidence of the mishap. We do have a wonderful neighbor handy-man, Roland, who was able to replace the element giving us the opportunity to do a thorough cleaning behind it, and we were happy we did not have to replace the stove.

- I also squeezed in dental, medical, nails and hair appointments.

- The Genesis was swiped by a hit and run at 'Publix;' checked on getting it repaired but was not worth it, so I bought a special color pen at the Hyundai dealership to hide the scratches.

*Bill and Anne Coleman's story: He is the water aerobics instructor and we became good friends, as well; they were loyal and helpful during each of Bill's health crisis, hospitable hosts in their rambling welcoming home, and fun companions during regular lunches at favorite restaurants.

In the news

March 1 - Florida governor DeSantis declares a public health emergency for the state:
services started being limited: restaurants and bars close, take-out orders become available in some restaurants, gatherings of ten or less, social distance - six feet or more – wearing masks and gloves; empty shelves in grocery stores - particularly toilet paper; 'Publix' to open at 7:00 am twice a week to cater to seniors – I made it once and got a huge package of toilet paper rolls, as well as paper towels and napkins. 'Publix' stopped offering 'free' coffee, minimizing infection, but that was a huge disappointment to me...

Our activities

On one of the beautiful spring days, a Saturday, I drove us to the port, ordered take out from 'Grills,' found a secluded hidden patio at 'Rusty's' and had a lovely and safe lunch by the water.
We then drove down Cocoa Beach, where all entrances to the beach were taped off and blocked, and the resorts and pier closed as well, resembling a ghost town.

Finally the state 'order' to close all non-essential business was placed to take effect on **Friday, April 3**; I was able to squeeze in my last hair cut on Thursday, just like I had the last manicure before Kenny closed voluntarily two weeks prior to the order (wish I had also done a pedicure),
Our occasional escape to 'Beef O'Brady's' or 'Lone Cabbage' became unavailable.

Back to the news

Crises discussions increase with shortages of tests, respirators, and PPE (Personal Protection Equipment).

As China's coronavirus cases diminish (**3/19** - no new cases) they increase in the US, which becomes the country with the most cases in the world on **3/27**.

The national leadership is disastrous: denial, misinformation; lashing out at the media; putting a completely ineffectual team in charge – other than the little Dr. Facio, the scientific expert who is ignored, but keeps his stance on informing us of the realities of the situation; making decisions that are completely irrational and having to change them; playing politics and favoritism with the governors depending on *"who is nice to him"* and the list goes on. **As someone said about the USA, facing the most terrible crisis of our times is made even more horrific by the least capable leader in our history!**

March 12 Black Thursday: the stock market collapses - Coronavirus crash; Covid recession; unemployment explodes rising in 29 states and DC.

March 23 – 'Kelly and Ryan Live' show begins being broadcasted from their homes side by side: she in Manhattan, he in LA side. This becomes the norm for all the shows that we watch regularly: TODAY, Stephen Colbert, and all others.

March 25 - Congress approves an unprecedented 2 trillion stimulus package.

On the societal level

April 15 - Adjusting to the new normal:

- no restaurants
- no movies
- no Elks, Moose, Eagles, American Legion, VFW, etc,
- no nails
- no hair
- no doctors, dentists appointments (only by phone)
- no gatherings with our kids or friends
- no audiences in televised shows: all broadcasted from the private homes of hosts/hostesses/guests

But ...

Our Activities

- I go to 'Publix' regularly wearing a mask (neighbors and friends make them and share them) and gloves.

- We take out from 'Beef O'Brady's,' 'Grills,' 'Pizza Gallery,' 'Pig'n the Whistle.'

- A few times we hide in a rickety patio from 'Rusty's' with our picnic lunch.

- We ride to Cocoa Village, order out in 'Ryan's' or 'Ossorio's' and find a bench or a picnic table to enjoy our lunch and wine (always wine).

- We take a ride in Tigger, our golf cart, through our park and me might stop for a glass of wine by the pool or join Hazel in the gazebo where we add some nibbles (last time was egg salad with sour cream and caviar).

- We sit under our tree or on the car-port and welcome neighbors keeping our six feet distance, but enjoy exchanging opinions and experiences during the pandemic!

- I have tried some new and some very old recipes: the dinosaur 'empanadas' in honor of Noah's first BD (which I sent in a cooler with dry-ice in UPS), a beef bone soup to dig out the 'caracú;' tripe, 'milanesas,' and I'll think of others.

- I try to join Candice in 'Zumba with Candice,' and do what I can (to Bill's entertainment and laughter), which isn't much...

- We have the support of the physical therapists Krista and Janice and the nurses Danielle and Terri, (always wearing masks) with phone reinforcement from Joelle, Dr. Antoine's nurse.

- We have Joe, the Barber, George, the pest control guy, Nancy, my cleaning lady and friend, who continue to come regularly, wearing masks to protect us, Bill in particular.

- We facetime with Savannah and Candice and participate in the activities of our great grandkids who get to recognize ABA and PAPI, in spite of separation.

- We also facetime, email, and phone Michael, our son, and Jenny, his wife, in Oregon, and Maria Paula our daughter, in Bradenton, to catch up with our daily events.

- We had a wonderful virtual birthday celebration for Savannah and Noah on Zoom: Savannah and

family obviously had to cancel the planned visit from New Mexico, but delighted in the video of family and friends vigorously washing our hands to the tune of HAPPY BIRTHDAY TO YOU, orchestrated by Madison. (This mimics the recommended length of time for pandemic hand-washing.) Noah was delighted to splash blue icing all over himself and Liam; loved the dinosaur 'empanadas,' not having to share with the party guests - one advantage to the 'virtual' celebration. Liam's critique of the 'empanadas' was; *"They are a little spicy, but I like spicy!"*

- We speak at length with Sissy (Bill's sister), Eduardo (my brother), old friends (Stan and Vera, Raquel, Julie, Lily, Mimí, Nené,..), and my family in Uruguay (Marcelo, Elena, Pablo, Carmen, Maggie...)

- Bill became a prolific artist, when he discovered an app on his phone that allows him to paint by numbers, and he entertains himself for hours.

- We look through our picture albums to enjoy them tremendously reliving different stages of our long and blessed lives, and...

- …to select photos to incorporate into my 'OUT OF THE MOUTH OF BABES,' which I continue proofreading and improving (I think).

In the news

We entertain ourselves and fret with the national and world news:

- In this unprecedented disaster, our 'leader' (DT) is the most corrupt, incompetent, egocentric creature, surrounded by sycophants of the same vein.

- Bickering with governors (democrats) and with his own 'experts,' including Dr. Anthony Fauci, the science infectious disease authority.

- DT announces that he wants to open up the country by Easter (April 12), *"because that is a beautiful day."*

- He dismantled the Pandemic Response Team which was created by Obama in 2018, but declared: *"I don't take responsibility at all."*

- The plague will go away very soon, *"his hunch."*

- Desperately needed testing and Professional Protective Equipment and Respirators he will provide at whim, to *"governors that are nice to him."*

- Retracts on the Easter opening under pressure from 'data,' and reality.

- DT promotes an untested and unapproved drug Hydroxychloroquine, which treats Malaria, against medical advice risking lives; stops Fauci from answering questions on the subject.

- DT insults and dismisses the media, while treating the daily briefings as his own political rallies.

- He is questioned about his original denial and delays in action which made the eruption of the epidemic so much worse. The timeline of his actions and inactions are well documented.

- Then, like a toddler, announces that the World Health Organization (WHO) is to blame and stops the funding in the middle of the Global Pandemic with international repercussions, feared even by some of his own followers in congress, which he ignores.

- Insists on having his signature on the stimulus checks that are beginning to be sent out.

- He then begins to consider opening the country for the economy and insists that he has 'TOTAL POWER' to do this regardless of Governors opinion.

- He had told governors that they should provide their own needs and Federal government had no responsibility.

- There are more than 36,000 deaths nationwide as of April 15.

- Some of his supporters begin to protest particularly against Democratic Governor Gretchen Whitmer of Michigan for her stringent lock-down measures. These people are carrying rifles, confederate flags, and block ambulances access to Emergency entrances.

- DT tweets to go ahead and "LIBERATE" from the Democratic governments, and considers those demonstrators "responsible people." A PRESIDENT INCITING THE POPULACE TO REBEL!!! **[Fast forward: precursor to January 6, 2021]**

- The three stage federal plan to open the country is a superficial guideline which does NOT include the basic needs of states: a coordinated commitment at the federal level to provide testing, PPE, and respirators as needed! We should use Germany as an example of effective response to this unprecedented global crisis.

- **April 24** - Latest: DT SERIOUSLY proposes in his CV 'briefing' to treat people with ultraviolet light or inject them with disinfectant!!!! Even Dr. Birx, one of his scientific advisors, was visibly flabbergasted, as was the medical community. LYSOL immediately published a disclaimer warning the public NOT to ingest their products!!!

April 27 – Recapping:

Gas prices are $1.55-$1.70.
Taxes are not due until July 15th.
The government sent us a stimulus check.
School cancelled - yes cancelled. Students are doing eLearning since 03/16/2020.
Social distancing and self-quarantining measures are on the rise.
Tape on the floors at grocery stores and others to help distance shoppers (6ft) from each other... isles are one-way with designated arrow signs; all wearing gloves and masks. It's like a movie.
Limited number of people inside stores; therefore, lineups outside the doors.
Non-essential stores and businesses mandated to close.
Parks, trails, entire cities locked up.
Entire sports seasons cancelled.
Concerts, tours, festivals, entertainment events - cancelled or rescheduled.
Weddings, family celebrations, holiday gatherings - cancelled or rescheduled.
No masses, churches are closed. Easter services were online and some pastors across the country were arrested for parking lot car services.
No gatherings of 50 or more, then 20, then 10 or more, STAY IN declared.
Don't socialize with anyone outside of your home.

Children's outdoor play parks are closed.

We are to distance from each other.

Shortage of masks, gowns, gloves for our front-line workers.

Shortage of ventilators for the critically ill.

Panic-buying sets in and we have no toilet paper, no disinfecting supplies, no paper towels, no laundry soap, no hand sanitizer.

Shelves are bare EVERYWHERE.

Manufacturers, distilleries and other businesses switch their lines to help make visors, masks, hand sanitizer and PPE.

Government closes the border to all non-essential travel.

Fines are established for breaking the rules.

Stadiums and recreation facilities open up for the overflow of Covid-19 patients.

Press conferences daily from President Trump.

Daily updates on new cases, recoveries, and deaths.

Government incentives to stay home.

Barely anyone on the roads.

People wearing masks and gloves outside.

Essential service workers are terrified to go to work.

Medical field workers are afraid to go home to their families.

This is the Coronavirus (Covid-19) Pandemic, declared March 11th, 2020.

In the news and in our personal lives

- The tug of war begins in earnest: demonstrations to demand opening the businesses include 'trumpsters' arms-carrying thugs, threats, and ignorance against the voices of restrain and reason based on scientific data.

- Stage One in Florida, thank goodness, includes Nails, Hair, and Restaurants, all with specific restrictions: social distance, wearing masks, 25% of capacity indoors, and active disinfection and hygiene.

- We had lunch at our neighborhood 'Beef O Brady's' and were happy that all restrictions were followed.

- We rode through Cocoa Beach after the beaches were open and then, again when the parking areas were also open, as well as some of the restaurants, all seemed packed.

- Maria Paula came to visit us for a couple of days; we met at the newly reopened Lone Cabbage Fish Camp, and were happy that the servers wore masks. We mostly enjoyed her visit at home, with Bill cooking 'choripans' and 'morcilla al pan' for me.

- We did meet *Hazel at the Gazebo for one of our Happy Hours.

- For Mother's Day weekend we decided to go to one of my favorites, 'Mainly Lobster;' the attention was wonderful and my lobster delicious, but none of the servers was wearing masks, and none of the patrons except Bill and I. We felt uncomfortable about this, even though we were seated outside and the tables had been distanced from each other.

- But on Sunday we decided to escape back to 'Lone Cabbage' and were disappointed that our server was not wearing a mask, although Norman, the owner, and his family were present.

- I was delighted to be able to get my nails, pedicure and haircut, and that the businesses seemed to strictly adhere to the protocols.

- **By the 15th of the month, there are 88,000 deaths in the US, the highest of any country in the world (nothing to brag about).**

- We finally got the yard signs we had ordered in favor of Joe Biden, and posted them proudly.

- In spite of the dismal performance of this administration in the face of this global unprecedented disaster, the ongoing blatant lies, the stupidities, the narcissistic and totally insensitive behavior of DT, he still has his following, which by its nature defines them, the enabling GOP, and disgracefully, our present society.

- Half way through the month, we began hearing about a murder of Ahmaud Arber, a black man, in Brunswick, Georgia, being shot on February 23, by a Father and son (McMichaels) while jogging, without any weapons. No charges were filed until reported, and in May a father and son were charged with murder, and eventually, also Roddy Bryan, a witness that appears to have chased and blocked the victim.

- On **May 25,** George Floyd, another black man, was murdered by a policeman chocking him with his knee on his neck for almost nine minutes, while Mr. Floyd was crying out "I CAN'T BREATHE." This led to unprecedented protests and riots throughout the country.

- Now, it is the end of **May, the 31st,** and the confrontations are chaotic. Blame is placed on extremists, on the left and on the right, but, of course DT blames the left wing, without evidence.

- The National Guard is deployed, curfews are in place, and the country is in total chaos...

- The opening of businesses continues, but the new crises are increasing the possibility of a second wave of Covid-19.

   * Hazel's story: She was the chorus director, which Bill was invited to join soon after we moved into Lost Lakes. We became friends and enjoyed outings with her and her husband Jerry. He and I were a supporting audience when Hazel and Bill shined in many a Karaoke performance! Unfortunately Jerry lost his battle with cancer two years ago.

On the personal level

- Candice and family planned to visit us: great excitement and care to avoid infection. All plans are in place when we have a call informing us that she had a minor accident, but was being charged and held in custody: bottom line we were supposed to send $14,000 to get her bailed out of jail. Last minute, when I was rushing out to the bank, she calls, and lets me know that they are on their way for their scheduled visit: *"What? You are not in jail?"* She thought I had lost my mind, but it was a close call to becoming the victims of the scam.

- Loved their visit; enjoyed the boys; Liam wore me out, but loved every minute of his wit, intelligence, curiosity, and humor. We had our happy hour with Hazel on the Clubhouse deck; the boys (that is Justin and Liam) fished and caught a lot of (10 or 25) fish which were returned to the lake, fed the turtles, while we sipped our wine and Irish Cream, accompanied by delicious spinach and cheese squares.

- The sad and very concerning news is that Justin lost his job. These are such difficult times that it is very worrisome for us.

- Another heartbreaking reality at this time is my brother, Marcelo's deteriorating health. I had calls from Pablo, my nephew and godson, as well as from Elena, his wife, keeping us informed. Not a very hopeful scenario. More bad news in this '**Annus Horribilis!**'

But a great contrast is the Historic shuttle from SpaceX beautiful and perfect launch from our Port Canaveral on **Saturday May 30** (which we witnessed in awe and amazement), arriving in the International Space Station 19 hours later!

June 6 - Forty six years since D-Day invasion, and hopefully...
'A week that will change the country and the world for the better.'

<u>On a personal level</u>

I found out from Pablo and Maggie that my brother Marcelo is practically in hospice, at home, with palliative care, not expected to survive the coming week. Thankfully, my conversation with Elena lifted my spirits, since she is accepting it, counting on their long life and love together, and comforted by the wonderful medical care he is receiving and by the support of their exceptional kids and friends. Anecdote: Elena's symbolic and esoteric conversations were noted by her granddaughter Olivia: *"Yo no te entiendo nada de lo que tu dices, Abuela"* (*I don't understand anything that you say, Grandmother.*) We are not even able to consider visiting since the border in Uruguay is closed due to Covid-19; no flights scheduled into the country.

- In Florida we are now in Phase 2 of openings, including bars, so we decided to go, wearing masks, to the Titusville Elks in the new rented location and meet Maxie and Clyde for a drink.

- Bought Chinese takeout for a change: huge portions, but a bit disappointing in taste.

- Continue our routines, using masks when we go out, trying to stay clear of big groups (never mind crowds), regular physical therapy (Krista and Janice with masks) for Bill.

<u>On a societal level</u>

- Demonstrations and protests throughout the country; BLACK LIVES MATTER, in unprecedented numbers have spilled into the rest of the world: France, Germany, UK...

- The news media alternates between the passionate but peaceful marches, and the looters and violent confrontations; incidents of police brutality continue to emerge while the demonstrations embody the demand for change and control of that same issue.

- As a contrast, law enforcement joins demonstrators in marching or in kneeling.

- Of course, DT only makes matters worse! Instead of empathy and understanding, of which he is incapable, he threatens to invoke the military power to invade the streets against the same people that they are supposed to protect and defend. Ex. Photo op stunt: St. John Episcopal Church with a scathing reaction by Bishop Mariann Budde about the abuse of the principles of the true faith to be used as superficial props! And lies, lies, lies:

Lie #1: The U.S. is banning all air travel from Europe.

Lie #2: The U.S. is banning trade and cargo shipments from Europe.

Lie #3: Health insurance companies will waive all co-pays for COVID-19 treatment.

Lie #4: Testing is expanding rapidly.

Some promises made and unfulfilled:

1. *Mexico will pay for the wall*
2. *I will release my taxes*
3. *I will sue my sexual assault accusers*
4. *I have a plan for better, cheaper healthcare for everyone*
5. *I will eliminate Isis in 30 days*
6. *I will not play golf or take vacations*
7. *I will eliminate the federal debt*
8. *I will bring back coal jobs*
9. *Trade wars are easy to win*
10. *North Korea is no longer a nuclear threat*

In the news

HUGE PAINTED SIGN IN DC ON THE STREET LEADING TO WHITE HOUSE: 'BLACK LIVES MATTER' IN YELLOW LETTERS. A kudo to the DC Mayor, Muriel Bowser.

Latest scandal: a 75 year old protester who was pushed by police, hit his head on the pavement and was left bleeding from his ears while they nonchalantly walked around him. DT, without any basis whatsoever (what else is new?), tweeted that he was an *"Antifa agitator,"* and that the fall seemed harder than the push, so this was probably a *"set-up."* Cuomo has the best response of all calling it *"dumb comment"* indicating that he should apologize and *"show some decency; show some humanity."* That is like expecting pears out of an elm tree! 'ANTIFA' stands for 'Anti-Fascism,' and is far from being an organized entity, much less a 'far-left terrorist group,' as implied.

Incredible times we are living in: global pandemic, unprecedented social discontent and unparalleled corruption in the US government.

On a personal level

- For my part, I cannot stop thinking about Marcelo with pain in my heart. I speak with Elena daily, but the waiting and the knowledge of the inevitable is deeply distressing.

- I also worry about Maria Paula during these stressful times, and about Candice and family with Justin's job concerns.

- We went to Lake Nona for a vascular test and will return Friday for Eye doctor appointment; we take the opportunity for nice different lunches: 'Hooter's' yesterday and planning on 'Columbia' in Celebration after Optometrist visit. Always with a mask!

- Actually, instead of driving to 'Columbia' in Celebration, further away from home (as I had planned), we ended up eating at 'Bonefish Grill' on Semoran Blvd (by the Airport); it was a good choice.

- Constant rain the first two weeks in June; struggling with roof leaks and trying to get them fixed.

- Had a good Book Club meeting at Hazel's with three new participants; no special recommendations for my taste, but I do have a pile of good potentials to read.

- Watched the movies 'Cats' and 'Little Women' at home; not great, but worth seeing.

In the news

The protests – 'BLACK LIVES MATTER'- continue worldwide, but acts of brutality against black individuals occur almost daily. This seems to be a worse epidemic than Covid-19. And, as expected with the opening of social life and the mass demonstrations there is a resurgence of new cases in many states, including Florida. No mention of this crisis from the White House; the administration has moved on to the new issue; of course, with little if any empathy, but threatening military attacks to the people of the US.

On a personal level

June 13 - The dreaded call came early in the morning: my brother Marcelo passed away, after a long decline and seven days in 'palliative care' at home. It was torture to feel so impotent and isolated from him; called daily and spoke with Elena, Pablo, and Maggie during the ordeal. We spent the day talking to our family and friends here in the US, particularly with brother Eduardo. I am so glad that I had gone to visit him a year ago, with Madison. TOUGH TIMES!!!

Dr. Maria H. Koonce

Mi hermano Marcelo ...

No sé si los recuerdos tempranos son mios o contados, pero ...

Veo a mamá con una sandía en el vientre.

Poco después, en el 'Hotel Hermitage,' con familia y amigos, en pleno despliegue de alta sociedad, el hermoso y redondito bebé en su sillita recitando la rima: " Es una vaca lechera, no es una vaca cualquiera... ES UNA VACA PUTA!"

Participando sin ganas en las puestas en escena de tantas actuacions teatrales inventadas por mí con nuestro hermano Eduardo y amigos del vecindario.

Disfrutando las dos semanas de verano en 'La Pension Reich,' en Colonia Suiza, con la sana magia del campo: recogiendo huevos; trepándonos a los árboles a recoger manzanas, membrillos, peras; tirando con asco los baldes de desperdicios a los cerdos en su corral; admirando a Ofelia seleccionar la gallina para la cena y retorciéndole el pescuezo con destreza y falta de resquemores; y sobre todo, los caballos, tirando los charretines, o ensillados para nuestro reto de noveles jinetes. Esta experiencia le sembró el amor de por vida por ese noble animal y asi disfrutó intensamente de sus haras, la cria de los mejores equinos, para lo cual aprendió el linage de cada uno con orgullo de padre.

Creciendo en un muchacho ambicioso y serio, pero con un sentido de humor rápido y picante.

Encomtró a Elena, su pareja de por vida, madre de sus tres hijos, compañera en las buenas y en las malas.

Y hubieron muchas.

Las buenas; parrilladas en sus haras en Colonia Suiza, con toda clase de achuras, y buenos vinos; lo mismo en Montevideo en el ubicuo Mercado del Puerto; las carreras de caballos en 'Maroñas,' alentando al suyo, el ganador 'Nahora,' con alaridos hasta quedarse ronco; el descubrimiento de los mejores restaurantes, o de algun arrabal donde intentábamos algunos pasos tangueros; las escapadas a Punta del Este o Punta del Diablo... Inolvidables festejos Navideños en familia, los Fines de Año, farreando hasta el amanecer, incluso el que Marcelo descubrió el gusto por Irish Whisky en un bar recien abierto de unos amigos en Maldonado y perdimos la cuenta de la cantidad que ordenó. Los viajes aventureros a la Argentina, a visitarnos en USA y por el mundo entero; el crucero por el Mediterraneo que hicimos juntos las dos parejas en Princess en el 2010.

Las malas: la trágica muerte de papá, que presenció en su adolescencia; la pérdida de un bebé, Nicolás; la de nuestra venerada matriarca; su diabetis; su dañado higado por la nefritis infantil; su internado por varios meses en el Hospital Británico en el 2015, que culminó con bypass coronario e infecciones. Por último el tumor en el esófago, que le incrementó la decadencia en su etapa final.

No hubo mejor padre, con ilimitada abnegacion por sus hijos, Marcelo Enrique, Pablo, y Maggie, todos profesionales, como lo fue Marcelo, todos respetados cada cual en su ramo.

Por otro lado, también fue hijo excepcional, siempre atento a las necesidades de nuestra madre con el avance de los años. ¡Un ejemplo de su lealtad es cuando se trepó de una terraza vecina a la de ella, en el piso 13 del Edificio Vogar, para rescatarla de una de sus frecuentes caídas!

Debo mencionar su placer por la música clásica; recuerdo una conversacion reciente sobre lo que habríamos cambiado en nuestras vidas, y su respuesta fue que él hubiera querido ser musicólogo profesional. Tambien su talento artisitico, ejecutando varios oleos impresionistas de escenas callejeras.

Otras cosas que compartimos y creo que nos enriquecieron a ambos, fueron los libros, discusiones de política global, y las expresiones intelectuales de todo tipo: entre conversaciones y recomendaciones en nuestras frecuentes charlas telefónicas (también en las ocasiones de encuentros), me inspiró a apreciar y disfrutar el genio cinematográfico de Woody Allen.

Mi hermano Marcelo y yo siempre tuvimos afinidad y cariño el uno por el otro, pero desde la falta de nuestra madre, desaparecida en el 2009, esos sentimientos se intensificaron notablemente en nuestra profunda amistad y respeto mutuo, que reconocimos y supimos expresarlos emocionalmente a través de la distancia que nos separaba.

Marcelo y Bill fallecieron con un mes de diferencia; Elena y yo compartimos tristes experiencias con mucho en común paralelamente. ¡Pero lo que mas se destaca es que tanto uno como el otro vivieron la vida con plenitud, intensidad y sabiduría, lo cual puede simbolizarse con la famosa canción de Frank Sinatra: 'A MI MANERA!'

ENGLISH TRANSLATION:

My brother, Marcelo...

I don't know if these memories are mine or told to me, but...

I see mamá with a watermelon in her belly.

A little after in the Hermitage Hotel, with family and friends, in full display of high society, the beautiful and round baby in his high chair, reciting the rime: "It is a milky cow, it's not any cow.... IT IS A WHORE COW!"

Participating without enthusiasm in the many theatrical performances invented by me with our brother Eduardo and neighborhood friends.

Enjoying the two summer weeks in 'Reich Boarding House' in Colonia Suiza, with the healthy magic of the countryside; collecting eggs, climbing trees to gather apples, quince, pears; throwing with disgust buckets of waste to the pigs in their pen, admiring Ofelia as she selected the chicken for dinner and twisting its neck with skill and lack of worries; and especially the horses, pulling the carts, or saddled for our inexperienced jockey's challenge. This experience sowed his lifelong love for this noble animal, and so he intensely enjoyed his horse ranches, the racing of the best equines, for which he learned the lineage of each one with a father's pride.

Growing up into an ambitious and serious young man, with a quick and sharp sense of humor.

He found Elena, his partner for life, mother of his three children, companion in god and in bad times. And there were many.

The good ones: 'parrilladas' in his horse-ranch in Colonia Suiza with all kinds of 'achuras,' and good wines; the same thing in Montevideo in the ubiquitous 'Mercado del Puerto,' the horse races in 'Maroñas', rooting for his, the winner 'Nahora,' with screams until getting hoarse; the discovery of the best restaurants, or some traditional dump where we tried out some Tango steps; the escapes to Punta del Este or Punta del Diablo... Unforgettable Xmas celebrations with the family, the New Year's Eves, parting until dawn, including the one when Marcelo discovered his taste for Irish Whisky in a brand new bar in Maldonado opened by friends, and loosing count as to how many he ordered. The adventurous trips to Argentina, to visit us in the USA, and around the entire world; the cruise in the Princess that we took together – the two couples – through the Mediterranean Sea in 2010.

The bad ones: the tragic death of our father which he witnessed in his adolescence, the loss of a baby, Nicholas; the one of our venerated matriarch; his diabetes and his damaged kidney by his childhood nephritis; his hospital stay during several months in the British Hospital in 2015 which resulted in a coronary bypass and infections. Finally the esophageal tumor, which increased his decline in the final stage.

There never was a better father, with unlimited abnegation for his children, Marcelo Enrique, Pablo, and Maggie, all professionals, as Marcelo was, all highly successful and respected in their respective fields.

On the other hand, he was also an exceptional son, always alert to the needs of our mother as the years advanced. One example of his loyalty is when he climbed from a neighbor's terrace to hers, on the 13th floor of Building Vogar, to rescue her from one of her frequent falls!

I have to mention his pleasure for classical music; I remember a recent conversation about what we would change in our lives and his response was that he would like to have been a professional musicologist. Also his artistic talent, producing several impressionist oils of street scenes.

Other things that we shared and I believe it enriched us both were books, discussions about global policies, and intellectual expressions of all kinds; between conversations and recommendations during our frequent telephone chats (and also during some of our encounters), he inspired me to appreciate and enjoy the cinematographic genius of Woody Allen.

My brother Marcelo and I always had affinity and love for each other, but since the absence of our mother, gone in 2009, those feelings became notably intensified in our deep friendship and mutual respect, which we recognized and were able to express emotionally through the distance that separated us.

Marcelo and Bill passed away with one month difference; Elena and I share these sad experience with much in common in a parallel way. But what is most outstanding about both is that they lived life fully, intensely, and with wisdom, which can be symbolized with Frank Sinatra's famous lyrics: 'I DID IT MY WAY!'

On the national level

The reopening of 'economy,' the ignorant reaction against using a facial covering as well as other health experts recommendations, has resulted in increase in Covid-19 cases and deaths in most states, including Florida.

We started more visits to restaurants and in most cases find to be the only ones wearing masks; the social distance is loosely observed with table distribution, but mostly servers are not wearing masks. In many instances it appears as people believe the pandemic to be over if it ever existed. This is particularly evident in the news media showing large gatherings in public places, night sites, and of course in the increased demonstrations throughout the country and the world. DT scheduled his first rally since it began, in Tulsa, Oklahoma, bragging about the millions of tickets requested and ordering a huge overflow to the facility. Thankfully, like all his inflated grandiosity, this did not come to pass: the overflow was removed and the inside facility photos showed a sea of 'blue' (empty chairs). Hopefully a sign of what will come to pass in November election.

Towards the end of June, we are facing a strengthening of the Coronavirus pandemic, with possibilities of local governments requiring use of masks in all public outings (already in effect in Orlando), and reversing the opening of activities and services to avoid a second wave feared by science experts like Dr. Fauci. Europe is considering banning travel for Americans. States like New York, which stopped being the epicenter, are banning entry from Floridians, who are quickly becoming the worst hit by the pandemic, in an ironic reversal. From the federal government, not a reference to this national crisis.

The national Administration's attention is now directed at the deafening cry for equality and justice of the 'BLACK LIVES MATTER' movement, but of course, on the wrong side. Recent cases of police and vigilante brutality like George Floyd brought about the focus on older ones like Trayvon Martin, and a massive movement to address this social evil.

In summary, this month of June has seen the expansion of the unprecedented crisis of Coronavirus to new dimensions, the caving of our economy, and unemployment not seen since the great depression, the monumental social unrest caused by racism and brutality, combined with an ineffective and corrupt administration, at times of political strife and division.

An overview of how unfit the 45th US President is to run the country, pend by my friend Raquel T. Manning, with which I totally agree, follows:

I question why the loving and just God I have come to know throughout my life, would allow our great land and its people to have such a disturbing and dangerous president? Mr. POTUS is making a mockery of the Constitution of the United States. He is the closest thing to a dictator we have ever experienced. There are so many things that come to mind to describe this presidents' personality and behavior that is overwhelming! I will point out some here that I have observed since he became president: Mr. Trump is a narcissist and a pathological liar (as of today May 28 he has said more than 18,000 lies or false statements). He is a racist, bigot as well as a self-serving man and a bully. He has been a failure in many of his business dealings, with at least four bankruptcies under his belt. He is vulgar, arrogant, ignorant, misogynistic, demagogue, egocentric and islamophobic. He is a divider who motivates hate and revenge, as well as being a xenophobic, with no compassion or empathy at all, (separating children from their parents and putting them in cages). His envy and hate towards President Obama is so obvious; he creates conspiracy theories (e.g., Obama gate) that divert attention from the real problems of the nation, like the deadly COVD-19 pandemic. He can't even humble himself enough to admit that he is wrong or made a mistake. He needs to read Matthew 23:12 "Whoever exalts himself shall be humbled and whoever humbles himself shall be exalted."

Mr. Trump is an adulterer and a sex predator, and regarding immigration he is a hypocrite; his mother, grandfather and two of his wives are naturalized citizens. His swearing and insulting in public must be a sign of something more profound—a need to show machismo or bravado—and that apparently appeals to his base and intimidates his minions in Congress. What happened to PRESIDENTIAL DECORUM? Mr. Trump has not been very successful in foreign affairs either. In dealing with Europa, his arrogance and lack of diplomacy has not set well with its leaders. How can he have good foreign relations when he insults them? As professor of international relations Stephen M. Walt said, "Trump most visible foreign-policy 'achievement' is a steady and sharp decline in America's global image." And what happened to his promise of fixing the infrastructure decay of this nation? (Streets, bridges, water, sewer system, public buildings, etc.), something he said it would provide jobs for lots of workers. Oh! But he blames, as a five year old would, somebody else, not his administration for why it has not been accomplished. The only building project he talks about is the "wall" which most Americans do not want, may never be finished and will not make us any safer. Last but not least, Mr. Trump has a disdain for the rule of law, science and the Constitution of the United States, which begs the question, what does he know? Is his lack of intellectual curiosity impeding him from learning how to lead the nation, and expanding his vocabulary or is he content to just constantly brag about himself?

Raquel T. Manning

<u>On a personal level</u>

Bill's health is declining, with persistent low blood pressure, but with permission from Dr. Antoine, his primary care physician, we did drive to Maria Paula's house to celebrate her birthday, her completion of her Bachelor's Degree in Nursing, Justin's new job at Lowe's, and Father's day. As always, we enjoyed the family, particularly the little ones; Liam exhausts me, but my physical, emotional, and physical exertions with him are well worth it.

Bill had two episodes of weakness in the legs, loss of balance, and disorientation, and Maria Paula was able to witness what I have been describing about these symptoms for two years. We saw his doctor, at her request, on Monday, and she concurs with the frustration of not being able to pinpoint a diagnosis; she and his cardiologist, Dr. Harris, requested a battery of lab tests and X-rays.

- As previously mentioned, we have been increasing our luncheons in favorite restaurants, combining medical appointments, which are also reappearing after being limited to phone consults for months. Haircuts and nails, also restarted with strict adherence to guidelines.

- We went with Hazel to the Bier Garden for a German escape, and she cooked a meal for us when we returned from Maria Paula's on Sunday Father's day.

- At home, we had to stop eating our lunch on our new furniture in the Florida Room, since by mid-morning, it becomes an oven. We have had record temperatures even before summer became official **June 20th**.

- We celebrated neighbor Joe Keller's 94th birthday with a decorated golf cart parade and a loosely choral rendition of 'For he is a jolly good fellow.' He was delighted with the sketch I did of him in his Navy uniform as a young boy!

- We mostly stay in, following our routine of watching the evening news at 6:30 pm, whatever TV program appeals to us, one of my Netflix movies, or when all else fails, back to the Dean Martin tapes, which we re-play sequentially.

- Of course, I never lack a book to keep me snuggled in my tiger covered reading chair.

- And Bill continues staying busy with his latest hobby, painting by numbers on a phone 'app.'

July: 'ANNUS HORRIBILIS!'

I LOST THE LOVE OF MY LIFE: MY 'GRINGO' IS GONE!

Tuesday July 7 - We got ready to go to the Lake Nona VA for two appointments: first with the technician to program and learn the workings of the I-pad they had sent us to process the new normal for doctors contacts, and second with another technician to test bill's breathing capacity, which, unfortunately, as expected, had not improved, and meant continued use of the oxygen machine. Bill was his usual talkative self, making jokes and teasing the techs. We stopped at the canteen for a snack, which he hardly ate, and a cup of coffee. We then proceeded to the entrance, where I left him in the wheelchair as I went to get the car (Bill had not driven since January 4th when he was admitted to Lake Nona VA Hospital with pneumonia and flu). As I pulled up, I noticed that a lady had gotten out of her van and was chatting and laughing with him. When he got in the car I joked with him: *"So you found someone to flirt with? She is very attractive..." "Why would I, when I have the best?"*

As we drove off, it started to pour down. I abandoned my idea to have lunch at 'Carrabas' on Semoran by the airport, and headed home, Bill helping me the whole way along with the emergency lights to navigate through the deluge. Debating what to do about lunch, I offered to make gnocchis at home, but he didn't want gnocchis. As the weather had cleared, we decided to stop at our favorite 'Lone Cabbage.' I insisted that he should take the walker instead of the cane, since every time we had gone out for lunch in the last couple of weeks he had needed help to get back in the car. I noticed that again he ate very little, and asked for a box for his patty-melt. He used the walker fine to go to the bathroom and back (*"I hate it!"* he insisted), but on the way out of the restaurant his body gave out (*"I am falling..."*) and he did! Our friends Denise (who suggested we should call 911, but Bill was alert and same scenario as many previous times), and her aunt Pat immediately called the big boys, who got him in the car and even offered to follow us home to help there. He was alert and giving me directions, but when we reached our driveway, it was evident that he did not have the strength. I called Jim, next door, but for once he was unable to get him up, and even stumbled back himself, so I run across the street to get Rudy, and also called the 'fall-assist' service through the police, which had helped us before. When I run back outside I heard his last words *"my knees"* and saw they were bleeding, as the two men were trying to hold him up. I went in the shed to get him some towels and then saw his drooling face: he was not there. The ambulance arrived and the paramedics used the pumping equipment on his chest repeatedly as I was surrounded by neighbors. He was alive but critical, I was told, and I called Maria Paula, and left to follow him to Rockledge Regional Hospital. After a long wait I was called in and Dr Pino told me that sadly the time his brain was without oxygen caused irreparable damage.

The next few days were torture that I survived because of Maria Paula, and Scott (who drove 15 hours from Indiana), as well as the girls, Candice and Madison, frantic calls from Savannah and Michael, and good neighbors. I spoke with Dr. Antoine, who reinforced what the nurses, the assisting neurologist, and my patient daughter tried to tell me, during the discussion about his living will, he had emphatically rejected the option to remain alive with machines: MY LOVE WAS GONE... on Sunday, July 12, I kissed him goodbye and we had to let him go. Maria Paula, Scott and Madison were with me.

The rest of the month was a blur: the funeral arrangements, phone calls, dissuading Michael from flying down, as well as Savannah and Sissy. Then we learned that Nicholas, Eduardo's son, was in a motorcycle accident and in a coma, the night before Bill's Farewell! The service was scheduled for Monday July 27. My friend Harry Huck told me it was the most beautiful funeral they had ever attended.

The front of the venue was set up surrounding the marble urn with the flower arrangement we ordered and the one sent by Sissy, Marvin, and Bruce. I had brought the two paintings I had done of Bill, the one of him 'Listening to Music,' circa 1963, and the 'Profile of Father and Son,' circa 1968, and also several of my memoirs to display. The mourners started arriving from the Lost Lakes Community, from the Titusville Elks and, of course, relatives and friends from around Florida. Everyone was surprised that soon the round tables on the salon were filled and we had to order more chairs and open the partition to the side enclosure. We were told that in the last several months services had held no more than twenty participants, and we calculated we had over fifty. The Funeral staff headed by Rachel Kabboord, was amazingly attentive and accommodating to our every wish. We were able to socialize with the soft sounds of 'Country Classics,' and enjoyed a variety of beverages, so I indulged in my coffee habit. The service was announced by the Funeral Director at 11:00 punctually. Rev. Ron Meyr began by having us join in prayer and then reading the obituary:

William J. Koonce, Jr.

William (Bill) J. Koonce, Jr. was 79 years young. He passed away on Sunday, July 12, 2020 in Rockledge Regional Medical Center, Brevard County, FL. Bill was born in Kinston, NC, and moved to Florida in 1976 after an eventful and adventurous young life.

Bill was in the US Navy active service for two years before enrolling in East Carolina University, where he met Maria, an exchange student from Uruguay. Their romantic encounter paralleled the story of Tony and Maria in the then Broadway hit, 'West Side Story,' except theirs had a happy ending. Bill and Maria married in Uruguay, and had their son, Michael, there. They moved back to the United States in 1965, and he completed his Bachelor's Degree in Industrial Engineering. The family expanded with a daughter, Maria-Paula.

After a successful career in textiles and electronics, Bill joined his wife in the field of education, specifically the Adult program of English for Speakers of Other Languages (ESOL) in Broward County, FL. He held two Masters Degrees: one in Business Administration and one in Teaching. They enjoyed a lively period in their professional life conducting trainings throughout the state and became known as 'Batman and Robin.'

The surprising and destructive visits from Hurricanes Katrina and Wilma to South Florida in 2005 were very persuasive: retirement to a less congested and exposed area led him and Maria to Brevard County. They moved to Lost Lakes, where they found friendship and camaraderie. In their book 'Retirement Rocks' they describe this stage of their lives: the activities and trips that provided them with rich global exploration and fun, always supported and encouraged by their family and friends.

His mother-in-law said of Bill: "Si no existieras habría que inventarte..." (If you did not exist, we would have had to invent you). Bill was a truly genuine person, literally incapable of pretense or telling a lie; he was loyal and faithful in all his relationships particularly to the love of his life, Maria; he was 'Papi,' not only to his two children but to the granddaughters, great-grands and generations of their cousins and pals; he had a quick and sharp sense of humor along with the warmth that comes from real, deep caring; he was the ultimate 'people person' (one very British friend once commented: "Bill Koonce can talk to the rocks!... And the rocks will talk right back to him!") He was passionate about music, a graceful dancer (the 'twist' was his specialty); a talented 'Elvis' himself, relishing his many Karaoke sessions and his choral performances in the Lost Lakes community.

'My Gringo Listening to Music' Painted by Maria Koonce in 1963

Bill is survived by his son, Michael, and wife, Jenny, in Oregon; by his daughter Maria Paula Corley, from the west coast of Florida, by Scott Corley; by his brother, Bruce Koonce, and sister, Marion Koonce Haines, and husband, Marvin, from Pennsylvania. His grandchildren are Amanda Turner, Candice Griego, Savannah Saxon, Madison Corley, Darby, and Brady Schrader, with their respective spouses/'beaus'. His great grandchildren are Alahna, Elijiah, Nyjiah, Liam, Noah Olivia Grace, and Branch.

We will bid farewell to Bill at the Life Event Center at Florida Memorial, 5950 South US Highway 1, Rockledge, FL 32955 on Monday, July 27 beginning at 10:30 am.

Rev. Meyr then spoke with affection and insight about Bill, since he had evidently done his homework, and was able to quote liberally from my autobiographies.

Scott began by reading Michael's words about 'Papi,' because it was totally out of the question to risk him traveling from Oregon to Florida with his health condition.

> *Thank you all. I, as we all do, love our fathers very much. They are the honor and integrity that we hope our daughters find. They are the love and passions that our mothers have had the privilege. They are the men we hope to become and be remembered as. I will endeavor to be remembered as the son and man that William (Bill) Koonce has molded! Papi is my template for greatness. I love you, but will never miss you. You are and always will be the best of me.*

> *Michael W. Koonce, July 26, 2020*

Then Scott continued the eulogies; he was very emotional but humorous, reliving his relationship with 'Papi' since his teenage years, quoting 'The DASH' by Linda Ellis, and relating it to Papi's well lived time upon this earth.

After the final prayer, we all enjoyed the famous sounds of Frank Sinatra's MY WAY, and I could have sworn that was my lover singing it to me as he had done so many times before!

MY WAY

And now the end is near
And so I face the final curtain
I've lived a life that is full
I've traveled each and every highway
And more, much more than this
I did it MY WAY...

YES, IT WAS MY WAY!

We were then directed to accompany the urn to the burial site for the Military ceremony, and were invited to return to the salon for a FAREWELL CHEER and partake of the buffet reception in my Bill's honor.

Life goes on, especially young life; we celebrated Olivia Grace's second birthday virtually, but I went to Maria Paula's for the end of July to celebrate, with the new protocols, Madison's 21's and Liam's fourth. The theme for Liam's occasion was 'sharks,' so I struggled to make a few of the 'empanadas' in the shape of the scary animals; then Charlie and I drove by the Griegos' house leading the parade with a chewed up banner decoration, and accepted the care packets to go. Liam said it was the best birthday party ever!

On a personal level

The fog stays on.

- I spend hours writing cards; 'thank-yous' and announcements, and speaking with concerned friends and the kids. Other phone calls include credit cards, Social Security, utilities, going to the bank, meeting with a lawyer with Maria Paula, and back with James at the Funeral Home for the stone markers and to organize arrangements for my interment. Down the very comprehensive check-lists, both supplied by the funeral home, and personally created by me.

- I read and watch TV.

- My Lost Lakes friends try to entertain me: mostly Hazel (happy hour at 'Coconuts'), Maxie and Clyde (lunch at the 'Merritt Island Moose'), Roland and Konnie (at their home). Hazel and I even went to the Cocoa Village theatre for a lively performance of 'Nine to five.'

- Continue routines like haircut and nails and having Nancy do my monthly housecleaning.

- As I mentioned before, the night before Bill's service, Nicholas (my brother Eduardo's son), had a motorcycle accident, no helmet and a DUI. He was in a coma and the prognosis was uncertain. I re-established contact with Sylvia, Nicholas' mother, and followed his slow recovery, but thankful that miraculously he came out of the coma and was mobile enough to handle his needs, and was even communicating with some difficulty; it was decided to let him stay for therapy and the same facility that had been treating him and then Sylvia and her husband picked him up to help him through further rehabilitation in their Utah home.

The highlight of my life in August was to meet with Maria Paula, Charlie, Madison with Robert, Candice and the boys at 'Miller's Ale House,' approximately half way between their home and mine to celebrate Bill's 80th Birthday. I took my friend Hazel with me. We all made it into a festive occasion, with wine cheers, good food, great service and a slice of cake with the traditional candle. They brought several spoons for everyone to partake, but Liam did the honors; at one point he must have felt the need to be hospitable and gave Hazel one of the clean spoons for her to be able to enjoy the last left-over bite!

I cry out to my absent love: ***"Why did you leave me?"*** And I hear the silence respond. Half of me has been ripped away!

Joke: A man goes to a bar, and orders: "One Corona and two Hurricanes" the barman obliges and presents the bill: "your total is twenty-twenty!" This references the Corona virus and the historic 'Marco' and 'Laura' that hit Louisiana in a rapid sequence on **August 23** of TWENTY-TWENTY.

In the news

The unprecedented circumstances permeate the news: increasing number of infections and death; controversy about wearing masks exacerbated by the idiotic DT, who refuses to believe the scientists, and continues to hold crowded unprotected rallies, the unrest and protests about police brutality and unjustified killings of blacks, both peaceful and riotous.

Both the democratic convention and the republican convention were held in August. I watched the Democratic performance with interest, with passionate and eloquent speeches by Michelle Obama, unsurprisingly by Barack Obama, and by Jill and by Joe Biden, as well as the endorsement by respected statesmen, like Colin Powel. I did not torture myself to listen to the Trump family members, and the shameful arms wielding couple who were the bulk of the speakers in the republican circus.

On a personal level

Much of the tasks that follow a death have been completed, so that left me with more of an empty space in my life. Neighbors and friends, especially Hazel, are very consistent in staying in touch. Hazel and I have gone almost daily to scout resorts in Cocoa Beach to plan a Christmas escape for her and her daughter Laura, and me considering three or four days on the beach. I ended up reserving in the Discovery Beach Resort, where Bill and I had stayed several times.

For Labor day weekend I went to Maria Paula's; she was keeping the boys and it was busy but delightful couple of days with them: always a challenge to keep them entertained, but I loved playing 'identify the countries' with the 'milanesas' I had made, teaching Liam again to assemble 'alfajores de dulce de leche,' and admiring Noah's newly acquired dancing steps. We did not leave the house, but it was a perfect visit; the trip back was a lot less stressful than the one going there and I made it in less than 2 and ½ hours.

My stay at the Discovery was bittersweet, as expected; I felt Bill's presence everywhere and then missed him with ripping pain; walking on the beach, seating on the balcony, a little shopping at 'Beall's', strolling on Cocoa Beach Pier, having a Lobster roll there and then going again with Hazel and Bunny, who came for lunch with me, were all therapeutic; I will probably do it again.

When I checked out on Saturday I killed a bit of time in Jetty Park in a damp and drizzly morning. I met *Maxie and Clyde at the Moose; they insist on continuing to be part of my life and helping me in any way, and I truly appreciate it. While we were having lunch, I had a call from Margarita, one of the Yaya's – a long standing group of Hispanic friends in Fort Lauderdale. She gave me the shocking news that Mimi had had a stroke! Mimi is eight years younger than I, a fire-cracker Cuban retired teacher, adored by everyone, very well deserved, and my adopted 'sister.' Another **'ANNUS HORRIBILIS'** punishment. Fortunately, like Nicholas, even though it was considered a significant attack, she is recuperating at home, and starting speech therapy.

*Maxie and Clyde's story: We met them not long after moving to Cocoa at the Elks Lodge in Titusville; we responded to a brochure advertising a trip to Alaska; over dinner they began explaining the advantages of that adventure; I finally interrupted: *"You don't have to give us a sale-pitch: WE ARE GOING!"* **That became the first of countless cruises and travels, with them as resourceful travel agents, which have tremendously enriched our retirement years!**

I had a message from James from the Florida Memorial Gardens, so we scheduled a meeting to close some details and see the new marker on Bill's tomb. **I find it harder and harder to pretend that he is still with me...**

I don't cook anymore, and notice some weight gain; going out to lunch, eating as hunger hits, carbs, very little physical activity (I hate walking now and facing the many signs and banners supporting DT in our community: very depressing!) So I tried weighing in every morning and noting WW's points, but with little success – no motivation.

The rest of September involved: dinner at the Colemans', Spanish classes for *Bunny on Fridays, doctors' visits for me now, Book Club Meeting at Hazel's (very spare attendance), facetime with Olivia Grace and with Candice and boys, phone calls to Sissy in PA, Elena, Maggie and Pablo in Uruguay, and enduring one day at a time! I had begun writing a piece about my brother Marcelo, which was hard enough to do, but when I lost Bill it became impossible. With Michael's encouragement, I did finish it; the emotion shown by the family members who read it made it very well worth it; I also abided by Michael's request to translate it to share with others; they are both included in the June section in this journal.

*Bunny's story: She was the first neighbor that came to welcome us when Bill and I moved in. She lives next door with her husband Walt, but he also passed away not too long ago. Bunny encouraged and helped Bill to get a position in the port on Sundays (mostly greeting passengers and wishing them *"a wonderful cruise")*, and gave him a ride home at the end of the day. We also found out how much we had in common, as teachers of adults, having coincidentally attended the same conferences throughout previous years!

9/22 – I held an open house to donate Bill's clothes; Hazel came to help me. Only Jim, my next door neighbor, remembered and took some shirts. We ordered pizza and closed shop, so I foresee the next few weeks collecting big trash bags to take to Goodwill. But before that, one other person wearing Bill's size is Bill Coleman, and he was happy and thankful to take a significant bulk, including the formal wear, and so was I.

Another story is that my primary care physician, Dr. Worsley referred me to a cardiologist because of chest pains and an abnormal cat scan. I mentioned the only one I knew who used to be Bill's cardiologist prior to us transferring to all medical personnel in the Lake Nona VA facility; he is from India, and his name is Gadodia, but I called him Dr. God. At the beginning of our relationship he was very detached, and showed no sense of humor, but in time he loosened up, and when we said good bye, he gave me a hug. I went to his office as a new patient; he was surprised, but remembered us, and again, welcomed me with a hug, violating the guideline for social distancing imposed by the Coronavirus. When I mentioned it, he justified it because *"this was a very special occasion!"*

Maria Paula came over and I invited Hazel, Jim and Linda, for dinner; first entertainment since before Bill's passing. It was a fall decorations, and a simple, but welcome menu (Caprese salad with peaches, paella with mussels, spinach pudding, corn meal bake, and cheese cake), and a very congenial visit; as always I was so proud of my daughter, and also of my friends and neighbors here in Lost Lakes.

The next day takes us into October: Maria Paula and I visited the Florida Memorial Gardens, stopped briefly to see James and then took an autumn bouquet and felt pride in Bill's Military marker.

We then enjoyed a relaxing lunch in 'Grills on the River', and signed a mountain of paperwork at David Presnick's, the attorney. She also took time to teach me some of the technical aspects of the 'smart phone,' the access to Netflix, how to play audio books in the Genesis, and other adjustments in my media. I feel like I am definitely stretching my brain to the limit...

In the news

Every few days a new drama is reported:

- Russians are paying bounty to Taliban for US Soldiers killed; the president was briefed on July 26, but denies having received information (does he read at all?) So far, (**9/30**) nothing has been done about it!

- He makes disparaging insults to military: *"losers and suckers"*

- **9/11 19ᵗʰ Anniversary**; I was at Discovery in Cocoa Beach when the news of Bob Woodward, a highly respected journalist, published a book with audio, proving that DT knew of the real threat of the Coronavirus in January 28ᵗʰ: but he decided (in his own words) to *"play it down."* I thought this would be the end. A president's lies and subsequent actions that caused (up to that time) almost 200.000 deaths should definitely be cause to remove him as a candidate for the presidency of the US of America. But not a dent is made in his popularity, at least encountering the signs and flags lauding him, on my return home!

- He continued to hold his notorious rallies of hatred (never ideas or policies) packing up his cattle in mostly outdoor, but one indoor event, no masks, no social distance and spitting out his ignorant misinformation: a vaccine will be very soon available, or something he called *"herd mentality"* (it is actually 'herd immunity') will take care of Covid-19! In another rally he states that Covid-19 affects *"virtually nobody!"*

- Another fall issue is the school openings; no guidance, or support, but he wants them open for live classes; so, of course, his puppet DeSantis, governor of Florida, passes the order. After scrambling to provide the best possible safe environments, many schools (in all levels) have to close back up and continue to attempt on-line instruction due to new outbreaks of positive testing.

- To add to our social crises, the worst fires in California and Oregon are causing chaos and tragedy. They came very close to affecting Michael and his family, as well as Eduardo (living in Oregon), especially the harmful smoke.

- Hurricanes keep multiplying and we are running out of names: 'Wilfred' was the 21ˢᵗ and then we started using the Greek alphabet: 'Alpha' was the 22ⁿᵈ of the season.

'ANNUS HORRIBILIS:' September 18

Death of Ruth Bader Ginsberg! This is disastrous, not only because of the loss of an icon 'Notorious RBG' but because it will allow DT and the GOP to steal a third seat in the Supreme Court, turning it into a majority conservative body for generations to come. RBG's dying wish told to her granddaughter was that her replacement would not be appointed until after the elections. Of course, you could not expect Mitch McConnell or DT to honor such. Within hours, Mitch McConnell, who blocked Merritt B Garland, Obama's nominee to replace

Scalisi, almost a whole year before election, announced that he would rush a nomination by DT immediately; and so they did: on Saturday **9/26** at the White House Rose Garden, Judge Amy Coney Barrett was appointed by DT and the date for the hearings was set for October 12. Based on her reputation, other than being a woman ACB stands against everything RBG stood for during her long life and legacy, likely to reverse Row vs. Wade, and the Affordable Care Act.

If you are not from the military, this picture could totally escape you. But let me show you what we saw, but might not have recognized. This is RBG's casket going into the capital building. The leader of the detail is the one with their back to you in the foreground. The leader of the detail will have the honor of standing as her personal guard as she lies in state. Notice the shoulder boards on the uniform - she is an officer. Notice the bun at the neck - she is a female, but that is not all. Notice the baby blue cord on the right shoulder - that is the indicator for "Infantry", a branch and unit she could not have been part of only five years ago. There is a Ranger tab and Airborne pin on the front of her uniform, in another picture, - she was the first officer and is one of only thirty women who have successfully passed one of the most physically demanding schools the military has, one where 50% of the men

drop out in the first week, one that is all but required for the highest levels of military service, one that until 2015 women were barred from. A funeral detail is about the honored dead, not those who honor them, however, it was no accident that *this* Ranger was leading *that* detail. Her uniform was a black robe, but the justice was every inch a warrior, and they know their own. They could not have found a better living example of RBG life's work.

- Thanks to John Blair for sharing these important details -

Other news discussed are the issues regarding a peaceful transfer of power, basic tenet of democracy, as DT continues to sow seeds of doubt in the validity of our voting, of course, without any factual basis.

September 20: It is official - 200,000 deaths in US

Another bombshell: **9/20** New York Times reported about DT's taxes and financial situation: $750 in Federal Taxes for two consecutive years (2016 and 2017), and 0 for others; $70,000 deduction for Hair Styling! Consulting fees to his own daughter, who is already earning salary for her 'work' in the White House. This scandalous and corrupt behavior including conflicts of interest and a huge debt to unknown foreign creditors, creating a possible national security risk, does not seem to affect his base in the least!... MIND BOGLING!

9/27 - First debate Biden and DT: **DEBATE DEBACLE:** Chris Wallace from Fox News, the moderator could do very little in the face of a capricious, bullying, acting like a toddler, constantly interrupting, insulting, and attacking completely out of context, not offering any serious content. Biden was admirable in his restraint and also in his rebukes: *"Would you shut up, man?"* On the other hand DT refused to denounce the 'white supremacists,' and on the contrary, literally egged them on. He keeps blaming the left (what he refers to as ANTIFA) for the recent social disruptions, when the facts show that the majority of them are caused by the extreme right. Overall this performance was SHAMEFUL but it appears to have significantly favored Joe Biden: GOD WILLING!

BREAKING NEWS!

10/2 - OCTOBER SURPRISE: Early morning announcement by DT; HE CONTRACTED COVID-19!!! As the events unfold, so does Melania, and several others and it is tracked down to the Rose Garden event to nominate Amy Coney Barrett, held (as shown by video) with complete disregard to the Pandemic, ignoring the strong recommendations of their own medical team! The ramifications of this unprecedented crisis are huge and hard to wrap your mind around it. That same afternoon, DT was taken by helicopter to Walter Reed National Military Medical Center in Bethesda, Maryland for treatment!

Treatments include:
- Remdesivir (Antiviral medication)
- Antibody Cocktail (Covid-19 treatment)
- Dexamethasone (Steroid
- Supplemental Oxygen
- Zinc
- Vitamin D
- Famotidine (Antacid)
- Melatonin (Hormone dietary supplement)
- Aspirin
- NOT Hydroxychloroquine (the miracle cure he promoted)

After conflicting and misleading updates from his lead physician, Dr. Sean Conley, at the head of the V of ten white coats, DT schedules a joy ride around the facility to wave at his handful of supporters (risking two security guards in the armored vehicle), and declares himself cured. He is flown back to the White House in Marine one, and plays the role of Mussolini, Hitler, and Evita Perón, waving from the balcony surrounded by flags: his personal touch and first action is to defiantly remove his mask, and then utters the worse possible advice to the American public:

True to form, DT's assessment of his infection does not reflect any sense of responsibility. His first words: *"We go among military, or law enforcement personnel, and they want to hug you and even kiss you... we have done such a good job!"*

In the W. Reed Medical Center, DT is treated with Remdesivir, Dexamethane, and Monoclonal Antibodies, some experimental and all recommended for extreme cases, which this is not supposed to be so; medical reports are misleading and incomplete: a lot of misinformation is being dissected ad nauseam by the media. In spite of the short video appearances trying to reassure the public, and his claim that he *"learned a lot"* about Covid-19, his actions contradict that assertion. He is incapable of learning or changing. He scheduled a 'joy ride' around the compound in a hermetically sealed vehicle to wave at the small group of supporters that had gathered with their signs and flags, flagrantly risking the health of the secret service agents. He then insisted on being discharged and was returned to the White House at 6:30 on Monday 10/5 strutting like a third world country's dictator both leaving W. Reed and climbing the stairs to the balcony of the WH, where he posed in front of the flags and his first staged action was to deliberately take his face mask off and put it in his pocket; another photo op! His message once more is to dismiss the horror and power of this disease that as of now has killed over 210,000 people in the US without the least bit of respect of empathy!

In the meantime more positive Covid-19 tests (34) are recorded of those surrounding DT, particularly those who attended the infamous Rose Garden event – the Superspreader - of 9/26. Melania and later Barron are among them. In spite of three senators supposedly needing to quarantine, McConnell insists on holding the confirmation hearings of Amy C.B. to steal RBG's seat in the Supreme Court prior to election. What a farce!

On a personal level

- I continue marking time; even though Bill is not next to me me as I try to reach out and touch him, like I did for so many years, the big painting in the new shadow box greets me each morning and tells me to go on...

- I have established a routine of meeting Bunny on Friday mornings to help her with her efforts to learn Spanish; Hazel had a reception for the group she organized for 'Home Alone' singles to network.

- I made regular empanadas (not dinosaurs or sharks) this time to take to Maria Paula's for the weekend events.

- Candice told Liam that Aba was going to attend his 'soccer' (aka 'futbol') game, and he immediately asked: *"And Papi?" "No, Papi cannot be there..." "But he will be in my heart!"* and he continued; *"in Aba's heart, in Mimi's heart... and everybody else's." "Not sure about everybody else,"* objected his mother; but Liam insisted: *"Well, Papi knew a lot of people!"*

- The weekend of our 58th Wedding Anniversary and three months of his passing was packed with family love and activities, including a meal to get to know Roberto's parents, Ana and José. 'El Gordito' (Noah) is now participating in dancing, smiling, throwing kisses, yelling **"ABA"** at the top of his lungs, and playing with me and Liam.

*Joyce's story: she is one of identical twins living in our community, who lost Dick, her husband of many years. Not too long after, she met a lovely attentive gentleman and they planned to get married, but he was diagnosed with cancer and passed away. We then noticed in the clubhouse get-together that Harold Johnstone, who had recently lost his wife Sandy, was paying proprietary attention to Joyce; soon she changed her last name to Johnstone. They lived happily for about six months, before he became sick. I attended his funeral mass with my neighbors, Jim and Linda, on **October 17th.**

I am tending to my health with doctors' appointments and continue trying to establish a routine of exercising and eating right. I enjoy my regular conversations with Elena; and others. Pretty obsessed with the coming elections, and currently with the SHAM process of hearings for the nomination of Amy Coney Barrett for the Supreme Court judge vacancy left by the lamented death of Ruth Bader Ginsburg!

In the news

"This process is without integrity." Sharon Jones, Naperville

However, the hearings went on, as scheduled, the week of October 12. Amy Coney Barrett proved herself to be less qualified and honorable than predicted: it soon became quite obvious that she did not feel it necessary to answer any questions (could it be that she knew her approval was a done deal?). Her excuse was that she could not have an opinion on *"hypothetical"* issues, even after Sen Amy Klobushar referred her to the very real statutes about the criminality of voter suppression. Asked to list the five rights defended by the first amendment, a question I had to answer 43 years ago when applying for citizenship, she mumbled four of them, but forgot the very crucial one in today's social panorama, *'the right for the people peaceably to assemble,'* which is actively being threatened by government regulations.

Instead of the scheduled second Trump and Biden debate **October 15**, we were regaled by two Town Hall style events run at the same time in NBC and CBS, since DT refused to participate in the 'virtual' format for the debate due to his positive Covid-19 diagnosis. Predictably, Biden gave concise and factual information in an intelligent and mature manner, while the other one was combative, regurgitating the same lies about his 'successful' performance in dealing with the pandemic, and this time he refused to condemn the dangerous conspiracy postures of 'Q-non'!!!

10/18 – Feds say they thwarted a militia plot to kidnap Gretchen Whitmer, the Michigan governor, blow some bridges in response to her firm position on protecting her state from the pandemic. Thirteen men were charged. Unthinkable, but not surprising, in our present climate: a precursor of what is to come...

My activities

I continue trying to establish daily routines:
- dermatologist
- gastrointestinal
- cardiologist: stress test/echocardiogram
- lunch out: Pier 200 in Titusville, and the usual hang-outs (by myself)
- 'happy hours' with Hazel; Spanish with Bunny, lunches with Bill & Anne and with Maxie. & Clyde
- met Karen from Perú, Bunny's recently acquired daughter-in-law: good dinner and visit with Bunny's family, and Loretta and Ernie
- hair, nails
- lunch and theatre matinee in Melbourne, with Hazel, celebrating her BD
- completed 'Out of the Mouth of Babes'
- watching the evenings news

- phone calls, facetiming

- gather Bill's clothes and deliver bags and bags to Goodwill

Interminable loneliness: **"Where are you?"**

In the meantime...

Back to the news

- As expected Amy Coney Barrett was confirmed in a sham strictly partisan vote 52 to 48 to replace RBG turning in her grave - BLASPHEMY!

- Another hurricane, 'Zeta,' attacked the gulf coast.

- A new surge of Covid-19: 99,321 new cases, and 2, 310 new deaths in USA.

- DT continues to hold rallies, sometimes three in a day, in total disregard of the science protocols, lying with glee: *"We are turning the curve," "the pandemic is over,"* and so on... In one rally in Pennsylvania, supporters were left in chilling temperatures waiting for hours to get rides back to the cars; in another in Tampa, they were fainting because of the heat! Such a caring humanoid!

- As the election approaches, TORTURE with constant ads, debates, and the irresponsible rallies, full of lies and stupidities.

On a personal level

Joining Hazel in the Lost Lakes parade tonight - **HAPPY HALLOWEEN!**

In the news

11/3 – Elections; elections; elections... **OFFICIAL ELECTIONS!**
Even though in different states, including Florida, early voting had begun, and was taken advantage of in unprecedented numbers, the official Election Day brought anxiety and high expectations. As predicted, no results were announced and bedtime was the best option for me; unfortunately I woke up in the middle of the night and I turned on the TV only to hear DT announce himself as the winner: disgusted, I cut the TV off and worried about my finances if deprived of my Social Security, likely to occur under him in 2023; at least I plan to avoid the every horror to face the scenario to come!

Fortunately, in the morning, the panorama was much more hopeful, with Biden ahead in the popular vote. We went through four torturous days counting the reported results: after being stuck in B 224 vs T 213, Biden finally obtained the required 270 electoral votes and peaked at 306 to DT's 232 A LANDSLIDE, in DT's own assessment when the same numbers determined his win in 2016. The popular vote showed Biden's lead by more than 6 million votes: Joe Biden was officially declared the President Elect and Kamela Harris the Vice-President Elect by the press on Saturday 11/7 by noon! It was 'The highest turnout in more than a century.'

11/19 - To date, the monster in chief has refused to concede and to allow his administration to coordinate with the President-Elect's team the traditional democratic process of the peaceful transition of power! In addition, the majority of GOP has remained silent, and in fact, complicit in this criminal behavior. Conspiracy theories are promoting fraud; these theories are completely baseless and denied by all responsible election officials; lawsuits are initiated, and dismissed by the courts, while he continues to claim that 'he won.' After counts and recounts and state certifications occurring, Joe Biden has 80+ million votes!!! DT is having all kinds of tantrums!!!

In the meantime:

- Surge in Coronavirus: over a quarter of a million deaths in the US
- Politicizing the use of masks and other protective measures
- Promising vaccines in the foreseeable future: Moderna and Pfeizer
- Hurricanes: 'ETA' and 'IOTA'

On a personal level

Saturday 11/7 morning, as I open my blinds I discover my two yard Biden signs were gone. I suspected *Rudy; called Roseanne president of the Lost Lakes Association, who, as usual, was useless, and then reported it to the police. Later that day, my neighbor Jim texted me that he had found my signs in Rudy's trash can. I am now reinforcing my locks and installing a camera and motion sensor lights on the carport.

*Rudy's story: he lived across the street with his mother Jonnie, and was one of the two neighbors I called to help when Bill had his heart attack, so my husband practically died in his arms. Unfortunately he has an emotional problem; he was taken to hospital, and rehab, but refuses to cooperate; his mother left after changing the locks, and he is now staying with another neighbor, Marcella, but getting in trouble in the community. In my case it has to do with him being a 'trumpster' and us the exact opposite!

That same Saturday afternoon I drove to Sanford and met *Julie Rivera and her daughter Rosalinda, for lunch in our favorite German restaurant, and spent the evening and next morning with them catching up with each other's' lives and reminiscing through our long history of friendship. We said goodbye after a lovely outdoor brunch at the 'Rooster.'

*Julie Rivera's story: we met in Uruguay when Michael was a newborn. Bill and I had left him with my mother to go swimming in the 'Polo Club' pool, where I saw a man bobbing around and I whispered to Bill: *"That man is the American Lieutenant who offered me a job but removed the offer when I let him know that I was pregnant."* My Bill was delighted to be able to socialize with (the other Bill) Americans, who immediately invited us to their home, and a glass of BOURBON (otherwise unavailable in my country). We became lifelong friends.

- The next weekend, I went to Maria Paula's since Scott had flown in for a visit, and in spite of Charlie being under the weather, we had the usual family fun, living through the stress of these times!

- On two Tuesdays, I invited a select small group of democrats DT haters, for a cheer and celebration. Different dynamics but same theme and discussion! We all needed this...

- I continued my routines through November: loooong month...

- Several SpaceX launches, and I lucked out to be at 'Water's Edge Café' after my 'Jetty Park' walk, with a young waitress fascinated by our space program, who guided me through the recovery of the booster as it was happening in front of us.

And I grieve…

"Grief is just love with no place to go." Jamie Anderson

Same feeling I had and continue to have for my father, my mother, my brother, Bill' Nanny, and other lost loved ones…

…but **overwhelmingly for my missing half!**

Then, it was THANKSGIVINGS, and the babies bring meaning to my life; we celebrated with the traditional dinner, and then with a fun luncheon at 'Whiskey Joe's' on the Manatee River.

On a personal level

My birthday: December 1ˢᵗ – lots of calls throughout the day. When Hazel phoned me to confirm our agreement to go out for dinner, I feebly tried to talk her out of it: *"It is too cold; it gets dark by 5:30..."* She did not take no for an answer: very firmly and final, she affirmed: *"Never mind; we won't go far; I have a plan."* So when my callers asked about my plans for the evening, I said: *"I don't know, but I have a very bossy friend, who has a plan!"* Sure enough, she had invited a small group of our closest friends for a dinner celebration at her beautifully Holiday decorated home... I was truly surprised but forgot to take a photo of her table. My 'birthday cake' was a huge sandwich mound covered in cream cheese, since she knows that I

"don't eat sweets." Trivia game, easy conversations, and cards with presents, which were almost entirely booze; I had a lovely time!

Maria Paula and Madison's visit: they came the next evening and we just chatted and relaxed; next morning we did a little Xmas shopping and went to 'visit Papi' and then for a bowl of soup at 'Grills.' As usual, they helped me with electronics, like the outside security camera app, and some tasks, like putting my tree together, which gave me incentive to decorate it and enjoy turning the lights on first thing in the morning until ready for bed, all the way till 'El Dia de Reyes' Jan 6, 2021 (which turned out to be a shameful 'day that will live in infamy' in the history of this country)

12/6 - Death of Tabaré Vazquez (1/17/40 – 12/6/20). He was president twice in Uruguay (2005-2010 and 2015- 2020), an oncologist by profession, who continued to practice medicine on Fridays while holding office, which demonstrates the stability of our society. He was a member of the 'Frente Amplio,' the socialist party in Uruguay, and extremely popular.

When I was telling my friend Nancy Lucas at lunch about this, she was curious about his first name: I explained that it originates from a Uruguayan epic poem by Juan Zorrilla de San Martin by that title – **TABARĖ** – and recounted the story of the 'mestizo' Indian boy with blue eyes; I reminisced about this literary masterpiece by perusing its pages and sending her a copy of my favorite verses:

Duerme, hijo mio, mira, entre las ramas
Está dormido el viento;
El tigre en el flotante camalote,
Y en el nido los pájaros pequeños.

Ya no se ven los montes de las islas:
También estan durmiendo.
Han salido las nutrias de sus cuevas;
Se oye apenas la voz del teru-tero.'

....

Cayó la flor al río.
Se ha marchitado, ha muerto.
Ha brotado, en las grietas del sepulcro,
Un lirio amarillento.

La madre ya ha sentido
Mucho frio en los huesos;
La madre tiene, en torno de los ojos,
Amoratado cerco;

Y en el alma la angustia,
Y el temblor en los miembros,
Y en los brazos el niño que sonríe,
Y en los labios el ruego.

Duerme, hijo mio. Mira: entre las ramas
Está dormido el viento
El tigre en el flotante camalote,
Y en el nido los pájaros pequeños...

12/8 to 12/12 – I checked in at the Discovery Resort, again, with trepidation; it had turned cold (by Florida and my standards), but Candice and family were scheduled to arrive and spend three days at the International Palms Resort close by. It was a very special time for me to enjoy each and every one with loosely planned activities: meals, 'Jetty Park,' beach, and the surprise thrill of witnessing, for them the first time, the launch of a SpaceX shuttle; a ball of fire speeding up in the black sky from the beach! Before they left to go back to Bradenton, I invited them and also a small group of my friends from Lost Lakes for an informal lunch of sandwiches and wine. Liam looked a little puzzled as they all congregated in the condo, but being considerate and polite, he whispered in my ear: *"Aba, why are there so many strangers here?"* But soon, both boys enjoyed slapping hands and chatting with their new friends. And I bragged about my Candice and her handsome Justin!

Saturday, after I checked out, I gave myself two BD presents: a shopping spree at 'Beall's' (where I was treated to a surprising and significant BD discount), and an early lunch at 'Mainly Lobster' with a Lobster roll and a cup of clam chowder!

I interject another story about Liam that Maria Paula told me. As a school assignment he had to ask three people what did they like best about Xmas: so his grandmother responded: **"FAMILY"** and continued to explain with the usual platitudes. Then Liam decided he would ask Papi, who is still very much in his heart. He did so, privately, and when Maria Paula asked him what did Papi say, he responded with certainty: **"DINNER!"** Amazing how in his short years, he so clearly understood his Papi...

Dr. God paid me a compliment *"You are doing well"* and a scare *"You don't want to have a stroke."* So he added another pill to the already increased dosage of medicines to keep the blood pressure lowered. So now I am officially an 'OLD LADY,' checking my blood pressure regularly at 'Publix.'

I did not avail myself of the 'grief counseling' referrals, but identify with poems and words, like those of Elizabeth Ammons, with some wise choices I need to be reminded off: succumb to sorrow or *"Do what they would want. Smile, Open your heart, Love... and go on."*

Back at home to the normal routines: nails, hair, TV repair, George, the pest control guy, Roland, for the heavy tasks that I was unable to complete. Then I accepted Maxie and Clyde's invite and found the directions to their home in Titusville for a lovely and hospitable luncheon, as well as unloading a suitcase with the last of Bill's jackets and other odds and ends for the Does' yearly yard sale. On Sunday I splurged again taking Hazel to 'Mainly Lobster' in Cocoa Beach and this time I did order the full (though the small) one pounder lobster and finished our outing in the Tiki Bar at the Discovery Resort with pleasant old fashioned sing-a-long!

The corrected version of my marker is finally installed: James sent me the picture. I am now ready to join him... if not for the pull of my amazing tribe and their rich new lives...

<u>On the societal level</u>

- Surge in Covid-19 cases
- 'Wannabe Dictator' refuses to concede
- Approval and dissemination of first vaccines against Coronavirus
- A new strain of Coronavirus diagnosed in the UK
- 'Food Insecurity'
- Massive Cyber-attack perpetrated by Russia
- Strong winter storms on the Eastern states

12/15 - 300,000 deaths from Coronavirus in the United States

But the 'Wannabe Dictator' totally relinquished governing responsibilities: in all his frantic tweets he never once mentioned the unspeakable horror facing our country. Instead he obsesses about the election denying reality and promoting wild conspiracy theories with totally unfounded charges of massive fraud. Of course sycophants follow through, namely Rudy Giuliani, in his new unrecognizable persona, bringing about 50 court cases, which are summarily dismissed. The most totally without conscience is Texas Attorney General, Ken Paxton, suing the states of Pennsylvania, Wisconsin, Georgia and Michigan (all key for Biden) to the Supreme Court which (even with the three infamous DT's nominees) immediately declared there was 'no merit.' The worst part is that 126 Republican congressmen and 17 governors signed on to this frivolous farce.

12/15 - Electoral College officially votes declaring Joe Biden President Elect. Mitch McConnell finally accepts the result; this should be the end of this unprecedented attack on the basis of our democratic institutions. Not so: the new dimension in the stubborn dementia of the 'aberration' in the White House and his more determined idolaters is considering declaring Martial Law, and finally turning our model country into what would have been inconceivable just a few years ago: A DE FACTO DICTATORSHIP!!!

Fast forward: The latest events, already in 2021 is a leaked one hour phone call from DT to Georgia's Secretary of State, Brad Raffensperger, to pressure him to 'find' 11,780 votes; even though he is a Republican he refused, and schooled DT: *"Your data is incorrect."* Now we learned that the Congress re-certification of the electoral votes, which is historically a ceremonial event will be challenged by a substantial number of Republican congressmen!!! WHAT HAVE WE BECOME???

THE UNTHINKABLE ACTUALLY HAPPENED: January 6, 2021 – Insurrection in the Capitol incited by the "deranged, unhinged, dangerous" traitor occurs – a shameful chapter in our history that cost 5 lives and will continue to spread its evil tentacles throughout our country.

12/12 - Pfizer Vaccine approval - **12/18** - Moderna Vaccine approval

12/14 - US begins administration following United Kingdom **12/6**; Russia **12/7**; Argentina **12/10**. Now the Wannabe Dictator comes out of hiding to attempt to take credit for this unprecedented medical miracle in speed *("If it were not for me, it would have taken five years.")* and efficacy (95%). This was quickly debunked by the scientific world; it was a development of historical proportions, due to the vastly improved knowledge and resources in the modern globe. Now distribution and administration will follow; the logistics seem unsurmountable: government medical officials established tiers: front health workers, age, assisted living, underlying conditions, etc. Now we question why Senator Marco Rubio, 49, one of the 'Trumsters,' who routinely downplayed the pandemic, already received the vaccination...

As we cautiously rejoice in this light at the end of the tunnel, we learned a new strain of the virus appeared in the UK and other areas, which if not much different in symptoms it is easier to transmit. This is resulting in chaos as many countries ban travelers from the UK during the busiest travel activity since the beginning of the pandemic. We are constantly warned not to let our guard down and to continue following the protocols for protection: masks, social distancing, washing hands...

12/21 – Second Stimulus package approved - long disputed in Congress - following the one in March.

Another **'Annus Horribilis'** crisis: 'Covid has wreaked havoc on economic stability and on food insecurity.' The media has focused on the longer and longer lines in food pantries with no end in sight: worst rate of 'food insecurity' in the US in decades.

The worst ever US government cyber-attack was uncovered by federal agencies which consider it a 'grave risk' and Pompeo blames it on Russia. Of course DT downplays and ignores it.

To add to the turmoil December brought fires and heavy rain to California, with new storms, snow and thunderstorms moving across the US.

COVID-19 - 2020

	Total Cases	Total Deaths
Worlwide	84.7 M	1.84 M
USA	20.5 M	350 K

<u>On a Personal level</u>

12/22 – Maria Paula got the Moderna vaccine, first dose; Michael got the Pfizer vaccine, first dose.

Christmas at Maria Paula's; the usual traditions – joy in the little ones and remembering our continued blessings...

The best day for me was Maria Paula's Birthday gift: downtown St. Pete for a girl's lovely lunch of 'tapas' at 'Ceviche's' and an incredible exhibit of Vincent Van Gogh art in the 'Salvador Dalí Museum.' In all my travels and museum visits I had never been so amazed and moved: the modern technology applied with incredible creativity and skill made it possible. For about 40 minutes in one salon his works came alive around us with music, words, and color.

I also enjoyed my private brunch as a Cougar, with my young date, Scott, at 'The Broken Egg,' and the movies we watched with Maria Paula.

New Year back in Lost Lakes with many phone calls and a small dinner at Hazel's.

Back to the News

On **Dec 21** there was a space phenomenon worth noting: Jupiter and Saturn came so close that they appeared to merge into one star. This last time this happened was 397 years ago and the next time is predicted to be 3/2080. It is called the 'Great Conjunction,' and identified as the 'Christmas Star,' which led the Wise Men to Baby Jesus. In 2020, hopefully the 'Christmas Star' is a harbinger of better years to come...

Other Books
by

Dr. Maria H. Koonce

Published by AuthorHouse

Loving the Gringo, A Bicultural Life, 2008

Six Tudor Queens, A Historical Play, 2008

Retirement Rocks, Life's Rollercoaster, 2014

An Extra/Ordinary Life, 2017

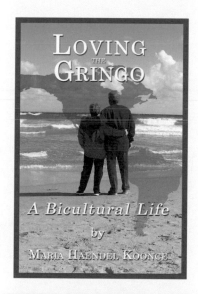

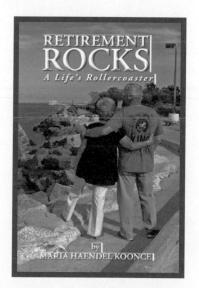

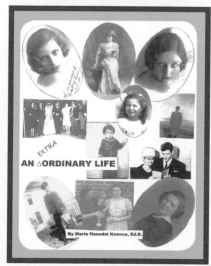

Printed in the United States
by Baker & Taylor Publisher Services